A New True Book

THE CHEROKEE

By Emilie U. Lepthien

CHILDRENS PRESS ™

CHICAGO

Cherokee mask carved out of wood

PHOTO CREDITS

© Michal Heron—Cover, 2, 12 (2 photos), 21, 31, 42, 45 (center)
© Emilie Lepthien—4, 7, 8, 9, 10, 11 (left), 13, 23 (right), 24, 39, 45 (left)
Oklahoma Historical Society—17, 23 (left), 26, 34 (top), 37
Root Resources:
© Loren M. Root—11 (right), 14
© Tony Root—15, 41 (2 photos), 45 (right)
Western History Collections, University of Oklahoma Library—19, 20, 28, 34 (bottom)
Maps by Len Meents—5, 33
Cover: Woman weaving basket

Library of Congress Cataloging in Publication Data

Lepthien, Emilie U. (Emilie Utteg)
  The Cherokee.

  (A New true book)
  Includes index.
  Summary: Describes the customs, way of life, and history of the Cherokee Nation, from its earliest days to the present.
  1. Cherokee Indians—Juvenile literature.
[1. Cherokee Indians. 2. Indians of North America—Southern States] I. Title.
E99.C5L38 1985   975'.00497   84-27476
ISBN 0-516-01938-4

TABLE OF CONTENTS

Cherokee still live in the Smoky Mountains.

A RICH AND BEAUTIFUL LAND

The Cherokee say the Great Spirit gave them their land. And what a beautiful land it was! Their territory was in the Appalachian Mountains. It covered parts of eight states.

Cherokee Land

A Cherokee legend says the Cherokee came from far away in the northwest. This may be true.

Centuries ago, people probably did come across from Siberia to North America. Some moved farther south and became the Indians of South America.

But many stayed in North America. The Cherokee formed one of the woodland tribes.

This herb and vegetable garden grows foods the Cherokee eat.

The Cherokee hunted in the forests. They fished in the cold mountain streams. They farmed in the valleys.

The Cherokee were hardworking, intelligent, and peaceful. They rarely fought other Indian tribes.

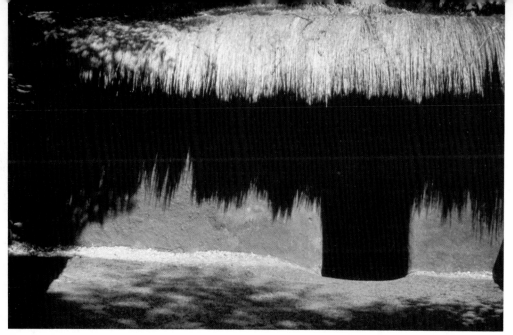

Some Cherokee lived in houses made of woven river cane.

CHEROKEE LIFE

The Cherokee who lived in towns built log houses. Others built houses of grass and mud. Wild grasses were used for the roof. Each house had a

The Cherokee built log cabins over two hundred years ago.

fireplace for warmth in winter. Although much of the cooking was done outdoors, the women could also cook indoors.

The work in a Cherokee town was often shared.

A Cherokee vegetable garden

There were town farms as well as family farms. The men prepared the fields for planting. Then the women planted the seeds and harvested the crops.

The land was rich. So the Cherokee had good

Cherokee crafts include working designs with colorful beads (left) and decorating pottery with tribal patterns (right).

crops of corn (maize), beans, and squash.

The women taught the girls how to plant and hoe and reap. The girls learned how to pound the corn to make flour. They learned to prepare food.

Basket weaving is another Cherokee craft.

In the fall the girls gathered nuts. They carried them home in baskets they had woven. They made pottery jars to carry water. Meals were served in pottery bowls.

Great Smoky Mountains National Park

HUNTING AND FISHING

The men hunted deer and bear in the forests. For large game they used the bow and arrow. The meat was shared by the clan. The women made clothing from the animal

Cherokee demonstrates how canoes were dug out with burning coals.

skins. But the men usually made and repaired their own moccasins.

Fish were also important. Many were caught by building traps.

The men cut down trees to clear the land for farming. To make canoes they hollowed out tree

Cherokee shapes an arrowhead.

trunks by burning them with hot coals. Then they scraped the insides with sharp stones.

The men taught the boys how to make canoes and bows and arrows. The boys also learned to hunt for food.

THE CHEROKEE NATION

No tribe learned the white man's ways faster than the Cherokee. By 1809 they had a National Council that elected a principal chief. Each town still had its own uku (chief) and council, too. They set up their own schools, too. Missionaries came as teachers. The children were taught in English.

This school for Cherokee girls was established in 1888.

By 1837, the Cherokee Nation adopted a constitution like the Constitution of the United States. It called for a general election of the principal chief and the second chief.

SEQUOYAH AND THE SYLLABARY

The Cherokee had never had a written language. But one man saw how important a written language was.

Sequoyah was born in Tennessee about 1775. His mother was a Cherokee. His father was a white trader.

Sequoyah never went to school. He never learned

Sequoyah, whose English name was George Guess, invented the Cherokee alphabet and system of writing.

to read or write English. But he saw people using what he called "talking leaves." He saw them make marks on paper. He knew that the marks were like spoken words.

Cherokee alphabet

1 A, short. 2 A broad. 3 Lah. 4 Tsee. 5 Nah. 6 Weeh. 7 Weh. 8 Leeh. 9 Neh. 10 Mooh. 11 Keeh. 12 Yeeh. 13 Seeh. 14 Clanh. 15 Ah. 16 Luh. 17 Leh. 18 Hah. 19 Woh. 20 Cloh. 21 Tah. 22 Yahn. 23 Lahn. 24 Hee. 25 Ss (sibilant.) 26 Yoh. Un (French.) 28 Hoo. 29 Goh. 30 Tsoo. 31 Maugh. 32 Seh. 33 Saugh. 34 Cleegh. 35 Queegh. 36 Quegh. 37 Sah. 38 Quah. 39 Gnaugh (nasal.) 40 Kaah. 41 Tsahn. 42 Sahn. 43 Neeh. 44 Kah. 45 Taugh. 46 Keh. 47 Taah. 48 Khan. 49 Weeh. 50 Eeh. 51 Ooh. 52 Yeh. 53 Un. 54 Tun. 55 Kooh. 56 Tsoh. 57 Quoh. 58 Noo. 59 Na. 60 Loh. 61. Yu. 62 Tseh. 63 Tee. 64 Wahn. 65 Tooh. 66 Tch. 67 Tsah. 68 Un. 69 Neh. 70 —— 71 Tsooh. 72 Mah. 73 Clooh. 74 Haah. 75 Hah. 76 Meeh. 77 Clah. 78 Yah. 79 Wah. 80 Teeh. 81 Clegh. 82 Naa. 83 Quh. 84 Clah. 85 Maah 86 Quhn.

One day he saw an old English spelling book. He studied it and found there were just twenty-six figures used to make English words.

Sequoyah drew more than eighty characters. Each character stood for one syllable. The

20

Today many Cherokee children learn to speak, read, and write in their own language as well as in English.

characters became the Cherokee alphabet, or syllabary. Sequoyah is the only person in history to devise a written language by himself.

NEW ECHOTA

The Cherokee decided they needed a national capital. So they started New Town in Georgia. Later they changed its name to New Echota. Chota had been an ancient Cherokee town.

The Cherokee sold plots of land in New Echota. They laid out streets. Then they put up government buildings, including a

Cherokee Supreme Court building at New Echota (above). Photograph of a pipe-smoking Cherokee woman with a child (left).

Supreme Court building. They planned a National Library, a National Academy, and a print shop. They felt all of these were important for the Cherokee Nation.

The printing office of the *Cherokee Phoenix* in New Echota, Georgia

The Council decided to buy a printing press with two kinds of type— Cherokee and English. Elias Boudinot was sent to raise funds. He spoke at churches.

He said the Cherokee owned 22,000 cattle, 7,600 horses, 46,000 swine, 2,500 sheep, 762 looms, 2,488 spinning wheels, 2,943 plows, 172 wagons, 18 schools, 18 ferries, and many good roads. He said the Cherokee were good, hardworking people.

Boudinot was successful. He raised the money, and the press and type were ordered.

Indian print shop, 1909

The newspaper was called the *Cherokee Phoenix—Tsalagi Tsu-le-bi-sa-nu-bi.* It meant "I will rise."

BROKEN TREATIES

The Cherokee had a problem with the state of Georgia. Georgians wanted the Cherokee land.

The Cherokee and the American government had signed many treaties. But the treaties were broken. The Cherokee lost more and more land.

Near New Echota, a Cherokee found gold. Gold!

Hundreds of settlers rushed to grab Cherokee land.

Hundreds of people rushed onto Cherokee land. It was the first gold rush in the United States.

Georgia wanted the gold and any other riches that were found. The state demanded that the Indians be moved.

The United States Supreme Court said the land belonged to the Indians. But President Andrew Jackson ordered them to move anyway.

The tribe was divided. Some wanted to stay. Others thought they should leave. The U.S. government said they could have land west of the Mississippi River.

On December 23, 1835, seventy-nine Cherokee

signed the Treaty of New Echota. They agreed to move.

Later, 15,964 Cherokee signed a letter protesting the treaty.

But the United States Senate passed the treaty by just one vote. The Cherokee would have to leave. Most of the tribe would leave for Indian Territory, part of present-day Oklahoma.

Painting of the tragic Indians struggling along the Trail of Tears

THE TRAIL OF TEARS

In 1838 armed soldiers
rounded up every
Cherokee they could find.
Eight thousand were jailed
until boats could take

them by river to Fort
Gibson, in Indian Territory.

They arrived there in
winter. They could not farm
for many months. Food
was scarce. They had no
warm clothing. The land
was very different from the
beautiful places where they
had lived before.

Those Cherokee left
behind voted to travel
overland to Indian Territory.
They marched through

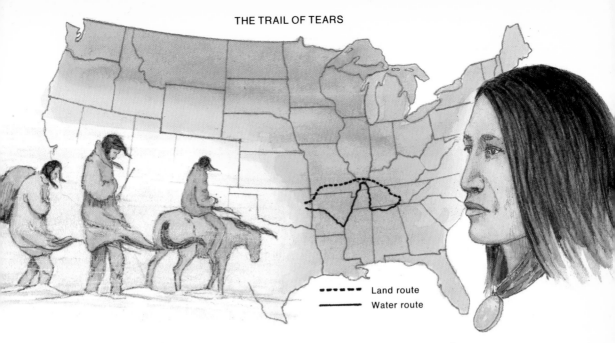

Land route
Water route

Nashville, Tennessee, and
up to Hopkinsville,
Kentucky. They crossed the
southern part of Illinois into
Missouri. They stopped at
Fort Smith, Arkansas.
Finally they reached Fort
Gibson in the Indian
Territory.

In 1903 W. C. Rogers, the last elected chief of the Cherokee (above),
addressed the Cherokee in their National Capitol in Tahlequah. The 1890
Cherokee Senate (below) also met in Tahlequah.

More than seventeen thousand Cherokee began the march. About four thousand died along the way. That is why the route has been called the Trail of Tears.

The western Cherokee nation set up its government in Tahlequah, Oklahoma. A Cherokee National Capitol was built. It has been restored and now holds a Cherokee museum.

OKLAHOMA

The Cherokee were not the only Indians forced to move west. Creek, Choctaw, Chickasaw, and Seminole were also moved to Indian Territory. Together they were called the Five Civilized Tribes.

Gas and oil were discovered on Cherokee land in 1904. The Indians were worried. They remembered what had

Chiefs of the Cherokee Nation included: top row, Lewis Downing, William P. Ross, Charles Thompson, John Ross; middle row, Dennis B. Bushyhead, Joel B. Mayes, C. J. Harris, Sequoyah; bottom row, S. H. Mayes, T. M. Buffington, and W. C. Rogers.

happened when gold was discovered in Georgia. They sent men to Congress to ask for an all-Indian state. They would call it Sequoyah. It would extend from the Arkansas border to where Oklahoma City is now.

Congress refused their request. In 1907 Oklahoma became a state. Indian Territory was part of the state.

Some of the Indians sold their land to oil men. They sold it very cheaply. Some kept their land and were paid for the oil on it.

In the east, the Cherokee National Headquarters are in Cherokee, North Carolina.

THE EASTERN BAND

About sixty Cherokee families lived in North Carolina. They were joined by twelve hundred Cherokee who had escaped being sent west.

Together they were called the Eastern Band. Today there are about nine thousand Cherokee in the Eastern Band.

Many of them live in Cherokee, North Carolina, or near Great Smoky Mountains National Park. Some depend on tourists for their income. Others have small farms along the Oconuluftee River.

They have set up a typical Cherokee village.

Weaving (left) and woodworking (right) are demonstrated in a model village.

Visitors can see how the Indians lived many years ago.

They also have a large outdoor theater. Each evening in summer they give a drama about their history and the Trail of Tears.

The older Cherokee teach the young about tribal history.

THE WESTERN BAND

The Cherokee in Oklahoma are called the Western Band. Some of the families in the Western Band receive money from oil on their land. Others have farms or raise cattle.

Like the Eastern Band, the tribe presents a play about the Trail of Tears. They too have a village to show their former way of life. They want to preserve their heritage.

The Western Band has 53,000 members. Many are still very poor. Principal Chief Ross Swimmer hopes to find work for his people in new industries.

FAMOUS CHEROKEE

There are many fine Cherokee artists. Franklin Gritts is a painter and John Julius Wiltnoy is a sculptor. Jerome Tiger and Robert Lindneux painted pictures of the Trail of Tears.

Will Rogers was a humorist who wrote about life and politics in America.

More and more young Cherokee have become

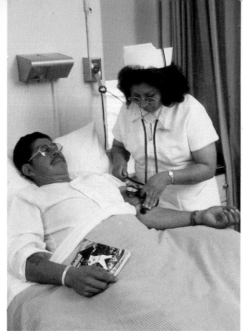

Trout farmer (left), nurse (middle), guide at the Cherokee village (right), combine ancient traditions with modern ways.

doctors, nurses, lawyers, teachers, and scientists.

The Cherokee can be proud of what they have accomplished. Today they keep their own rich culture while they work in the modern world.

WORDS YOU SHOULD KNOW

alphabet(AL • fuh • bet) — a set of letters or characters used to spell the words of a language

character(KAIR • ik • ter) — a symbol used in printing or writing a language

clan(KLAN) — a group of families, usually related, that live together

constitution(kon • stih • TOO • shun) — the basic laws of a nation or group of people

culture(KULL • cher) — the behavior and beliefs of a particular race, religion, or social group

election(ih • LEK • shun) — the choosing of a person, by voting, for a particular job, office, or position

festival(FESS • tih • vil) — a celebration that features special events, games, entertainment, food, etc.

game(GAIM) — wild animals that are hunted as a sport or for food

heritage(HAIR • ut • ij) — a culture or way of life passed down by parents and other ancestors

hoe(HO) — to weed or loosen earth around plants with a tool (called a hoe) made for the purpose

missionaries(MISH • un • air • eez) — persons who travel in order to spread religion

moccasins(MOCK • uh • sinz) — soft leather shoes without heels

pottery(POT • er • ee) — things made of clay, such as bowls, pots, dishes, etc.

protest(PRO • test) — to object to something by word or deed

reap(REEP) — to harvest a crop by cutting it down

scarce(SKAIRSS) — lacking in quantity; the opposite of plentiful

sculptor(SKULP • ter) — one who makes statues or other works of sculpture

stockade(stah • KAID) — an enclosure made of wooden posts and stakes, usually for holding prisoners

swine(SWYNE)—a type of animal, including pigs and hogs
syllabary(SIL • uh • burr • ee)—a set of characters that represent
        the syllables, or sounds, of a spoken language
treaty(TREET • ee)—an agreement made to promote peace
tribe(TRYBE)—a group of people of the same race and with the
        same customs who band together under one leader

INDEX

About the author

  Emilie Utteg Lepthien earned a BS and MA Degree and a certificate in school administration from Northwestern University. She has worked as an upper grade science and social studies teacher supervisor and a principal of an elementary and upper grade center for twenty years. Ms. Lepthien also has written and narrated science and social studies scripts for the Radio Council of the Chicago Board of Education.

  Ms. Lepthien was awarded the American Educator's Medal by Freedoms Foundation. She is a member of the Delta Kappa Gamma Society International, Chicago Principals Association, and life member of the NEA. She has been a co-author of primary social studies texts for Rand, McNally and Co. and an educational consultant for Encyclopaedia Britannica Films.

CHILDRENS PRESS

50495

9 780516 419381

ISBN 0-516-41938-2

A New True Book

THE SENECA